23
Ways to Sex Play

The Erotic Tales of Two Lost Souls Reunited

By: Chevella Dyer

Co- Author: Virgil Lindsey

Copyright© 2019 By: Chevella Dyer

Published 2019 By: Chevella Dyer

Copyright © <2019> by <Chevella Dyer>

All rights reserved. This book or any portion thereof may not be reproduced or used in any manner whatsoever without the express written permission of the publisher except for the use of brief quotations in a book review or scholarly journal.

First Printing: <2019>

ISBN <978-1-79477-138-3>

<Arts Love of Anything and Everything>
<3359 Eisenhower Cir>
<Atlanta>, <Georgia> <30354>

www.artsloveane.com

Table of Contents

1. Kiss Play
2. Fore Play
3. Mind Play
4. Smell Play
5. Memorial Play
6. To Do Play
7. Outside Play
8. Birthday Play
9. Anything and Everything Play
10. Water Play
11. Party Play
12. Ferris Wheel Play
13. Crazy for the Dick Play
14. Back and Forth Play
15. Daylight Play
16. We Got it Bad Play
17. Storage Play
18. New Home Play
19. Fantasy Play
20. Driveway Play
21. Storm Play
22. Dress Up Play
23. 23 Is Us Play

Dedication

I dedicate this book to all the lovers / freaks all around the world. Young, old, sneaking or being true. Get it in. Do You.

Signed,

Mr. Daddy's Little Nasty Girl

Introduction

There once was a young old lady who lived in stayed in the house with what felt like millions of peoples, yet somehow was always lonely and blue. Married yes, this part was also true. Unhappy in every way you can possibly imagine. Then one day along came Mr. Daddy, Saint Villo DeVille, my knight in shining armor to save me, to dry my tears, and kiss the pain away.

So, sit back and listen to our story of where it all began. Where two separated souls somehow manage to find each other again in this lost universe. But somehow, someway we found our way to each other, when we are not even looking, it just happened.

Now If you like nasty things and I do mean nasty, then you've got the right book. I hope you enjoy some of our 23 Plays.

"NO KIDS ALLOWED"

"PROCEED WITH CAUTION"

"BEWARE"

"XXX RATED"

Chapter 1

Kiss Play

Well, well, well... How do I start? With a kiss that changed my life in everyway. It took place on a cool Tuesday evening in Covington, Georgia. I was at a Mexican restaurant with my favorite Auntie on a lunch date. It was going fine until she made the conversation all about her. To be honest, it's always about her and only her. (So Boring) Aunt G is just chat chat chiggie chat chatting away, on and on and on. I have no clue what she is talking about. I am zoned out in my own little world. Then my cell phone rings. I hear his ring tone and I know exactly who this is, my insides warm up and I smile as I answer it. Before I can even say hello, I hear Saint V's voice. "What the business is, are you trying to smoke something with the kid today?" I say, "You already know. I am on highway 138 at the Mexican spot down the street from my house eating lunch with my Aunt. Come thru...pull up on me." Saint V says, "Bet."

About 15 minutes later he pulls up outside. I stare at him as he stares at me while I walk to the car. As I get inside, he says "Hey sexy, how are you?" I told him, "I am better now". He has a blunt of kush rolled up and he passes it to me to light it. We talk as we smoke until the blunt is gone. Now the conversation is flowing, we are getting to the good topics. All of a sudden, in the middle of my sentence, he kisses me. Not too hard, not too soft, yet ever so sweet and gentle. WOW, POW, BAM!!!!! THANK YOU, YES SIR!!!!...

Have you ever had one of those? I mean it takes your breath away, make you smile, scared, and confused all at the same time. What the f just happened...Emotional Overload. I jump out of his car and run back into the restaurant. I drop down in my seat speechless in shock. Aunt G keeps asking me, "What is wrong with you?". All I can do is smile and blush lost in La La Land. Until the next time I see him.

Now, what events led up to this surprise kiss? Why am I not pissed off at him? I am a married woman and he is not my husband. He did not ask my permission to kiss me. Why do I feel so drawn to him? The way he looks at me with true desire in his eyes makes me smile and giggle. Let's go back to the true beginning of when this all started. We met while he was hustling in the grocery store parking lot in Covington. He was in his car selling music and movies. My mom, my sister and I were going to get groceries to cook for my family. My mom, two sisters, two brothers and my niece live with me and my husband, my stepson and our two babies are all in the same house. He stopped us and asked if we needed any CDs or movies. He told me his name was Saint V and introduced myself," I am Red this is my sister and my mama. I looked at his list and we chatted for a few minutes. Someone called the police on Saint and they pulled up on us with the lights on. He finessed the police officer that pulled up on us while we were talking. The officer blocked his car then got out and asked if he was selling bootleg movies. Saint V said, "No officer, my name is Saint Villo DeVille. I am the CEO of D-Boy Music Atlanta. I am promoting my music and letting people hear and buy my cd. Do you have time to listen to my music right quick?" The officer left and we continued to talk. This man is too smooth. I bought some DVDs from him. I took his number so I could buy more movies later. We began to talk on the phone often and he came by my house frequently. Soon, I start ordering movies from him every day. I hate watching T.V., too many commercials.

Chapter 2

Fore Play

Days turn to weeks; weeks turn to months we have been shopping with each other talking and texting. I sold bud, so we started swapping out. We haven't had any deep conversations, but I really enjoy talking to him. One night I decide to hang out with one of my girlfriends at her house. She called over some extra company, people that I did not know. Everyone is chilling, smoking drinking and playing cards. Some lame ass guy kept trying to talk to me and feel on me. Before I knew it, I snapped on him. I put my finger in his face and looked him dead in his eyes.

"I have told you a few times already boy I am good." As if…. He is so drunk I don't know if he has heard anything that I have said, yet alone even see me straight. This fool too funny. Shortly after, that he was back in my face again asking me if I would like to go in the bedroom with him. My instincts say punch him in the eye. But that is not lady like. I am working on my temper but really, I can't take this no more. Since I don't drive, I am in a tough situation. My girlfriend is too wasted to drive me home. She is doing nothing to stop her company from harassing me, some friend. I take a deep breath, politely get up from the card table and walk out to the front porch.

I can't believe this, I got to call Saint V. The phone rings a few times and I expect the voice mail is about to come on. Then he answers, "Yo what's up sexy lady." I ask him where he is at. He replies, "Out here hustling up this paper. What's good witcha?" I don't know why but I said, "Come see me." Without hesitation he said, "Bet I am on the way." I told him I was not at home. He said, "Oh really." I said, "Yes really, I'm going to text you the address", and we hang up.

I walk back in the house and go straight to the bathroom to be alone. I'm leaning on the counter scrolling through FB until I get a text that reads, "I am outside." I walk out and get in his car. He is already smoking because he bought a bag from me this morning. He passes me the blunt and turns the music down as I start to talk. "Let me tell you about this ugly lame ass boy in there. He kept touching me and talking to me after I told him I am not interested." Then, I smiled at Saint and said, "That's why I called you, to come protect me." Saint gave me that side eye glare and leaned in close to me, "Oh that's how you feel?" I grabbed his hand, "Yep, come on in here and chill with me. I really don't want to be at home right now. I am not about to call my husband over here, he is one of the main people that I need to be away from." Saint replied, "I feel you, I am not ready to go home to my girl either. We used to be cool, now it seems like we're two roommates who can't tolerate each other."

We go back into my girlfriend's house chill and sip as we finally have a long talk face to face. Not texting or a quick phone call and not making a play. I think to myself, "Nice, I like this." During the conversation we found out that we are both in the entertainment field. He is a music artist and actor and I am an actress and a model. Oh shit!!!.... Let's get it... Open mic's together is where you can find us. We start performing music and stand-up comedy together live on stage. That's just some of the time, because Saint V is several different people in one. Saint Villo DeVille is the entertainer, but Virgil Lindsey is too many things. He is skilled in many trades and runs his own businesses.

First off, he is a certified electrician. Now when I found this out, it was shocking and amazing. I just had to see it too believe it. I was like a kid at Christmas. Like, "Oooh show me." I was so excited and overjoyed to know this and really had to see it. If you did not know the truth. It was a black man who discovered how two create a light bulb. So, shout out to Lewis Howard Latimer. R.I.P. and thank you Mr. Latimer. I thought to myself, "So this young black man can make light, let me see!" And just like that I was now his helper, tool girl, water girl, light girl, yeah that was me. After one job, we went straight to an open mic to perform his music at the club inside of an internet radio station. Guess what? We were live on the radio. I even got the chance to hit the stage and do one of my poems. When I was finished, I walked off the stage and hugged Saint. I am floating by now, on top of the world. He tells me I did a great job. People are shaking my hand and telling me they loved it.

It feels so good to be out in the real world, doing real stuff and sharing my talent with people. Years have gone by full of cleaning, cooking, baby sitting and being the maid for my entire household. None of them ever speak to me unless they want me to buy something or cook something or SMOKE SOMETHING. My husband was no different. We hardly ever said anything to each other now days. That's why being with Saint is so fun. Saint and I have a real connection. We are just friends at this point, but we are closer than me and my husband. I can talk to Saint and ask him anything. He made me discover the star inside me. I was so excited to see the crowd's positive response to my poem. I had to tell somebody. Saint had walked off talking with one of his boys, so I called home to check on my kids and tell my husband what I had just done. R. says to me, "You got what you want." I say, "What are you talking about?" R. says "Him. You want him you got him, so stay where you at." Then the phone hangs up. I guess…

Saint walks up with a drink for me and says congratulations. He looks into my eyes an he can tell that I am upset. He asked me if I am ready to leave and I said yes. We finished our drinks and left the radio station to stop at a restaurant for wings and fries. We take the food to this big building that is closed. He parks and we walk up the stairs to the door that he has the key to. He unlocks and opens the door as I hold the food and drinks. We step inside and he turns on the lights. I am stunned again. It is his massage studio. The lobby is beautiful. He rents a room here, that is why he has the key at 2:00 a.m. Ok, Ok, Boss Status! He is a certified massage therapist as well. It is so nice in here. I mean like a magazine picture. Everything is new and organized so neatly. I am truly impressed with how he has decorated his suite.

After we ate, we continued to talk. I started to open up and tell him about some secret personal stuff. I can't remember the last time anyone gave me their undivided attention and really listened to me without interrupting me. At some point I started crying. He sat beside me and wrapped his arms around me and wiped my tears away. He hugs me tightly until I compose myself and then walks out of the room without a word. He returns with a foot soak massager full of hot water. He takes my shoes off and puts my feet in it. He lets them soak for a little while then starts massaging them. He tells me that he understands the way I feel and that I good woman and mother. He calls me a "Thug Barbie" and says that I am a real survivor. He commends me for taking care of so many people for so long. He was actually listening to me and thinking about what I was saying. As he spoke, I felt like he was giving me the "thank you", that I yearned to hear from my family and friends. He rubbed all my pain and stress from my whole body through my soar, tired feet. Then used his organic sugar scrub to exfoliate them before he rinsed them and massaged them again. I never had a foot massage before. This is heaven.

Saint tells me that I deserve to have someone that will take care of me back. I deserve to have my feet and my whole body massaged on a regular basis. He dries my feet off and puts my shoes back on. We stand up and I stare at him as I cry tears of joy the first time in my life. He looks at me, leans into me and kisses my tears and then my forehead and then hugs my tighter than I have ever been hugged. I can't breathe, but I don't feel like I am suffocating. His cologne is intoxicating. I am so relaxed, like putty in his hands. He kisses my neck and says, "Don't worry. I got you. But it's time to take you home right now though."

Chapter 3

Mind Play

I am sitting outside on my front porch waiting for Saint V to pull up so we can go hit the block and hustle. I see his car coming down the street and I get a grin on my face that makes me laugh. It is something about this guy. Damn! He has his window down as he pulls into my driveway. I say, "There he go, hey sexy" He says, "Hey Gorgeous One." That's another new nickname he gave me. "I missed you." I respond, "Not as much as I missed you." Now I remind you, at this point, the kiss that I began the book with has not even happened yet. We are just friends. No sex, no titles, no pressure. Just two good friends taking care of each other. Yet this is how we talk to each other. I love that shit. True he gave me my first foot massage ever. True he is always on my mind. True he is the only person to ever hold me and let me cry on them. He makes me feel safe and important and valuable. I never met my Dad, so I have missed out on love and attention as long as I can remember. Saint makes me feel cared about like a good Dad would do for his daughter. He is concerned about my safety and well being. Every time he would see me walking, he gave me a ride. If he called me and I was walking he would come find me and pick me up. My husband and my mom just let me walk everywhere even though they both had cars. I always look forward to seeing Saint. We get along like we have known each other forever.

He asks me if I am ready, I say, "Yep, lets ride." We hit the block for a few hours and make some plays. We have smoked four blunts and now I am hungry. I say, "Craig". He says, "Smokey". Now, these are the two pet names that we use all day every day. Ya'll already know we smoke a lot. I say to him, "Do you know what I need now?" He replies, "Yep, you ready to eat." I say, "Bingo. How you know?" He said, "Because I am hungry too." We are near one of our favorite restaurants, so we pull in. We order, get a table and start talking as we wait for our food to be served. We ate some wings, Philly Cheesesteaks and fries with sweet teas to drink like always. Then went back to the spot, his massage suite. We burned two more on the way there. Before we get out the car,

Saint tells me to go into the bathroom, undress put on a robe and come to his suite. No questions asked I did as I was told, not knowing what was waiting on me or what was on his mind. I can't believe I feel so safe with him. As I walk out of the restroom and get closer to his door it opens and he hands me a glass of wine. "For you pretty lady, come on in."

I can now smell incense burning and see candles burning. I can hear the sound of waves splashing in the ocean and birds chirping. I am blown away. He has strawberries dipped in chocolate with whip cream. He is feeding them to me as I sip my wine. He is spoiling me and showering me with compliments. By my second cup of wine I was tipsy. He is teasing me with the whip cream and chocolate. He is telling me to just lick and suck off of the strawberry don't bite it. Then he says, "Now nibble it, yeah nibble it and suck the juice. I can tell you like that," as we lock eyes and smile. "Now give me this glass and lay on down. Let me rub your troubles and stress away."

From the first touch of his fingers on my bare skin, I felt my body melt. All of the troubles of life simply eased away. His hands feel so damn good to me. His energy is soothing me and energizing me at the same time. He is working my shoulders and arms, my hands and fingers, then returns to my shoulders and slides his slick, strong hands achy down my back. Thank You GOD! Yes, I have needed this my whole life. His fingers are magical. He keeps leaning closer to me as he massages me. What the..,? Those are his lips, and that is his tongue. He is kissing and licking my back. Oooohhh he so kinky. He continues until he covers every inch me with kisses. He is teasing the juices out of my Aquafina wet, wet. He is sending hot vibrations through my whole body. I have never felt like this.

This is blowing my mind. Now my legs are shaking, my eyes roll back in head and my whole body starts to tremble, out of control might I add. I was stuck in a trance. Something was happening to me and I did not want it to stop. "O.M.G", I am yelling and stuttering, "What, w w what are you doing to me?" With out any contact to my private parts he gives me a tremendous full body orgasm. I lose control completely and I start crying again. With tears of joy on my face. I can't help but thank God again. He pulls me up from the table to the sitting position. He stands in between my legs and pulls me tight to him in a long embrace as I sob and giggle. I am still coming, and he is laughing at me as he kisses my forehead softly again and again. My mind is racing. This could be it. Am I ready? Do I really want to do this? It's not the right time. I can't do it! Well, I guess he hears the thoughts in my head. Because Saint V says, "It is time to take you home." On the ride home, I am right back in la la land. I am thinking to myself how did he just do me that way? He never once touched my kitty cat, yet he still made me cum more times than I ever have before, back to back to back. He did this with no penetration at all. I am so in love and I am so afraid of that.

Chapter 4

Smell Play

Things are getting weird now. I have started telling lies to my family, friends and my husband, that's right. Straight like that. OK, I know that I am married. But SO WHAT!!! I have been unhappy for ten years trying my best to do everything right. I have never cheated on him. But I know he has cheated on me numerous times. I spend every day in the house cooking and cleaning for eleven people. Three kids and eight adults plus. His other kids and his family some of our neighbors and friends all ate when I cooked. I was the only person who cleaned up. I took all of our laundry to the laundry mat washed it and never got so much as a thank you from any of them. No one ever asks if I am good, or if I need or want anything? I have let people live with me because I too know what it feels like to be homeless. I have had to live with people a few times as well. So, helping and caring for people is not the problem. But I want some gratitude. How can I be taking care of eleven or more people every day and still feel lonely? That shit sad. How can I be so nice and caring to so many people for so many years and it takes this stranger to make me feel more appreciated than anyone in my life ever could. The conversations that we have seem to heal my pain. His words give me the strength and confidence to face tomorrow with hope and expectations for great things.

I finally have something to focus on to avoid being depressed and lonely all the time. So why should I feel guilty. It is not my fault. I deserve to have someone in my life that cares about me, not what I do for them. I have been deprived of love and attention my whole life. Now, I am trapped in a marriage with two babies that my husband does not even want. He already had seven kids before we met. What was I thinking about? I guess I got the leftovers. He can barely last five minutes on the rare occasion when he can get hard enough to put it in. I am so disappointed and sexually frustrated. I need some, BAD!!! And I need it to be REAL GOOD!!!! We don't even sleep in the same room no more. I sleep with my Autistic son and my daughter. My son is a hand full so when King don't, sleep Mama don't sleep.

Since my I was six, taking care of my family has been my responsibility. Now I am taking care of his family and mine. I need these getaways with Saint V just to stay sane. I have been making everyone around me happy my whole life. No one has made any effort to make me happy except for Saint V. For once in my life I am going to make a choice that makes me happy. It is time for me to do me. If it is wrong, then wrong is right. So, what do I want? I want my friend to be my man. Oh yeah….

I am so hot and bothered every time I talk to Saint. Just the sight of him makes my kitty jump. This shit is CRAZY!! Every time I leave the house, I am calling him to meet me even if it is just for five minutes, I'll take it. At least once every day, I need to see him, hug him, smell him. We met at the library and the grocery store. My mom has started helping me sneak to meet him. Some days he would take me and my kids to the park so they could play, or he would meet us up there and we talked and played with my babies. I have made up every story possible to sneak away and see Saint. When I am with him it feels like I have gone to another world that is peaceful, calm and secure. Even when we are working or hustling, we are still having fun.

I text Saint and ask him to bring me some new cartoon movies one day while my husband was at work and my kids were at school. I was fresh out of the shower with some tight thin red boy shorts on barely showing my little booty cheeks at the bottom. My perky titties look so sexy, nipples are rock hard pressing against the fabric of my wife beater, no bra. Am I setting him up? Maybe?

His ring tone comes through my phone and I answer it on the first ring. "Damn girl, you betta be ready to see me. I am in your driveway." I say, "Yes definitely, come on in the door is open. I am in my room." I am laying across my bed looking at the television. Looking extra cute for no reason, or am I? Hint Hint. Saint sits down on the bed as he hands me the movies. I say, "Thank You, young man. King is going to be so lit when he sees this new Ice Age. He loves him some Ice Age." He sits on the bed and watches the movie with me as I roll us a blunt to smoke. After the blunt is finished he lays his head on lap. At first, he is just watching the movie but having his face that close to my kitty made her start leaking with wetness. I could smell it and I know he could too. He even got closer and closer, until his nose literally was in my crotch. He opened my legs and sniffed and smelled me like he was giving me kitty cat inspection. It lasted for a while too. He was really, really, smelling me with deep breaths. I am speechless, just lying there trembling. He looks up at me and tells me how much he loves the smell. Then he pulls my shorts to the side and slides his tongue straight into my kitty cat slowly. He licks, it smells it and presses his whole face in it. He keeps licking my lips and clit slowly and gently then he pokes his tongue back in me and licks the juices up. I can't even hear the T.V. anymore. All I hear is him licking, kissing, sucking and slurping and me moaning. He tells me that I smell and taste so good. I am losing my mind all over again. My toes are curling, and my eyes are rolling back in my head again. I wasn't ready....No, No,No,Yes,Yes,Yes..... This is only the beginning of our 23 Ways of Sex Play. I hope you like it so far. We are just getting started.

Chapter 5

Memorial Play

He got me sprung and I can't deny it. Now I am thinking to myself, "What can I do to BLOW his mind and make him mine?" I also want him to know that I have never cheated on my husband before, so this is a really big deal to me. Guys have tried to talk to me before, but I always stayed true to my husband. Saint V is different though. We are close friends already this is not a booty call situation. This is a real relationship and a friendship. R broke his vows and I forgave him. Now, it is time for me to get my needs satisfied. I got to let Saint know that this is no joke and I am not playing. This is not a game. It's about to go down. Memorial Day 2014 is getting close. And Oh Yeah! I promise you it will be a day to remember.

So today is the day. It came faster than I anticipated. Today will be one of the most important days of my life. I am taking a huge chance, choosing my feelings over my marriage. But Saint makes me feel so good. I was not even looking for nobody when I met Saint. I was content with my life. I had been so busy taking care of everybody to realize how truly lonely I was. But my eyes are open now and they can't be closed again. I can see clearly now. So, Are you ready? Ok here we go. I am packing my bag. What do we have here? Long, blonde, wig check. Sexy red and black lace pantie and bra set, to die for, check. Heels check. Perfume check. Candles check. Music check. Yeah that's right, that way. Your girl is not playing. Yeah, he got me turned out, but this means "WAR!"

He picks me up and we head back to his apartment. The roommate is out so yeah, I tell him on the way there that I am going take a shower at his place. He said, "That's cool you know you are good." I smile at him and say, "I know I was just letting you know baby." After we go inside, I get comfortable and say, "I will be right back. Go ahead and roll up and put us a movie in, better yet roll three." As I walk to his bathroom to take my shower. He said bet and started rolling. After I turn the shower off, I can smell the loud and I hear the music on the movie began. Now I am fresh out the shower standing naked looking at myself in the mirror as I dry myself and put on my scented lotion and a dash of perfume. Let's slip on the secret weapon and prepare my surprises that I have packed. He is still in the living room, so I tip toe into his bedroom and set up the candles and turn the music on low. Then I call out to him, "Baby can you come in here. Bring the drinks and the smoke."

As he walks in, I am dancing very slow and seductive standing on his bed. He walks up to the bottom of the bed. I get on my hands and knees and crawl to him with my booty in the air. I say, "Hey Sexy". All he can say is WOW! What is your name? I said, "I'm White Chocolate, your friend Red sent me to give you your early birthday present. Just in case she does not get to see you on your birthday." "Thank you, sexy lady", he replied. "My pleasure, Mr.", I said back. "Just sit down, sip your drink, smoke and enjoy the show." I dance all around the room for him. From the bed to the floor to his lap. He grabs me and rubs his hand all over my body. He caresses my neck, my back, my shoulders down to my breast. My back is against his chest. My booty is in his lap. His fingers are in my panties sliding in and out of my dripping wet wabbit. I keep dancing but I am getting scared again at the same time. Can I really do this? As I move, I begin to cry. I whisper in his ear, "I need this so bad, but I do not want to get hurt. My heart can't take any more pain. Don't use me and get rid of me. Promise me it will not be only this one time. Can you promise me you will keep doing this to me and making me feel like this? I'm sorry I am not stalling I just don't do this I've never cheated on him before. And really it is not even about him exactly. It's the fact that I am a wife period. I know this is a dangerous decision to play with. I know that I want you, but I have to know that you honestly want me as much as I want you."

He has taken his hand out of panties; he is softly massaging my thighs as I confess my fears to him. If you can't guess by now, I am crying my heart out again. Really? Yes, a hot mess. He turns me around in his lap and holds tight me in his strong arms and kisses the tears on my face. Saint says, "baby bae, bae, look at me. Its O.K. Yes, I want you. I promise you I want you. I will definitely give it to you more than once. You don't ever have to worry about that. I promise you that! Then he stands up from the chair and picks me up and places me back on his bed. He positioned me in a comfortable pose and kissed every inch of my body. After rubbing kissing licking and sucking my everything, I feel my orgasm building back up for the third time as he slides the hardest dick ever in me. It is so stiff and hot, and he is sliding into me slowly with care and patience. I am so wet he is stretching my tight walls out with ease. This is so much better than all of my fantasies about him. I can't believe how he is filling me up completely. It hurts so good. I am screaming and crying but he keeps stroking slow, deep and gentle. Long pauses on the in stroke pressing my walls to the limits before he pulls halfway out and falls back in it again. He keeps kissing my ear and neck as he pumps in and out of me. Here go the tears of joy and I am squirting everywhere. I hear myself screaming but I can't believe it is me. Crazy huh? I am actually enjoying this. He is making slow love to me and I am screaming, "Oh my God Oh My God what are you trying to do to me." I am really losing my mind. I can't control anything at this point. He has total control over me, my mind, my body and my very soul. He makes slow passionate love to me for hours in every position he could think of. Then he held me as I fell asleep with my head on his chest.

Chapter 6

To Do Play

After that first time… Saint completely blew my mind. Now there is no way I will be without it. I have to have it, seriously. No joke, dead ass! My new Bae was the #1 thing to do on my to do list while my husband is at work and the kids are at school. If I am wrong, then wrong is right. Things are heating up quickly. We are worst than rabbits, I mean some days we do it 3 or 4 times. We have no shame, anywhere is the right place: car, shower, couch, bed, floor, countertops. You name it we did it. Yep, this is way past crazy. I do mean crazy. Geekin and freaking. I have to have it. I can't get enough it is so freaking good. Oh my God that man is amazing.

We have a habit of texting each other all night long if we are not together. So, one night we texted each other until about 2 a.m. He tried me and told me to come outside. He was outside waiting for me. He thought I was going to give him excuses. I texted, "Everyone is asleep except for me. I am on my out there." We ride out, park and we go in. After 3 orgasms I am back at home in time to wake my husband and kids up, feed them and get them out to work and school. Once everyone leaves, I cook breakfast for me and Saint V. So, it is one hour after he dropped me at home, and we are back together chilling smoking and eating this good food I just cooked. I served him scrambled cheese eggs, turkey bacon, waffles, orange juice and coffee with a side of head to go.

Have a great day Mr. Daddy. See you soon. I miss you already. I would find any way possible to make him a part of my daily to do list. It was just a must. We continued to meet at the library grocery store and the park. It could be few minutes to just smoke and chat face to face. Even if it was three hours together every second of it was exciting. Every time we made love it was better than the time before it. Our bodies needed each other in the worst way. Our attraction grows stronger with every touch. It felt like he had an intense hold on me or possession over me and I loved that shit! I could just think about him and I am soaking wet. He got me so gone my bold ass made his ring tone, "Your My Little Secret" by Exscape. Every time he called me, I would let the phone ring a few times before I picked up just for giggles. Too bad R is so clueless that he never caught on. Man, he so slow.

Chapter 7

Outside Play

One night after I get King and Angel to sleep around 1 a.m., I call up my Bae. I was all in my feelings because I did not see him that day because he had school and work. I ask him with an attitude, "Uhm can you come get me and fuck my brains out again." He like, "Bae you know it's 1 a.m. right?" I say, "Yes I do. The tables have turned. Are you down or are you gonna make me wait on it? I need you sorry." Saint says, "You don't ever have to be sorry for wanting me Gorgeous One. I will be on my way to you soon." When I get in his car, he asks, "Where are we going." I say, "I don't know. How about in the car again? Saint says, "We not about to park in a random spot like last time." I reply, "Let's park behind your apartment." He said, "You know my roommate is home, right?" I say, "Yeah and?" He calls her roommate, but they used to be more. I forgot to mention that part. She is the live-in ex. For shame, for shame.

So, we pull up behind his spot and we waste no time. First, we got in the back seat. By the first ten minutes we are hot and sweaty. I say, "Roll down the windows bae, I'm about to faint." We do it some more with the windows down and then I say, "It is still too hot, we got to get out of the car." Now we butt balls ass naked in his back yard. He got me on the hood of his car drilling deep inside me like this the last pussy on earth. He turns me around doggy-style and slaps my booty cheeks. I hear the echo as I moan. My love juice is running down the hood of his car and we are in our own world.

We don't care that we are outside in a residential area with apartments and houses all around us. We don't care that she is right inside. We don't even notice her walk into the kitchen at first. We have our eyes closed because our faces are covered in sweat. We both looked up and the light was on and she was in the refrigerator. We looked at each other and did the mannequin challenge. I guess we think this gone make us invisible.

But did we did not stop fucking, though? HELL NAWL. Ain't no way we bout to stop now. Shit.... She got her late-night snack and left the kitchen. The full moon shining bright and has us acting like animals. We moved to the lawn chair. I stretched out on my side and he raised my leg into a split and straddled me like two pair of scissors. My knee was pressed up to my ear and he was pounding me fast and deep. Then back to the car for two more positions. Those mosquitoes ate us up for hours. We continued to make mad, nasty, passionate love until we dosed off for a minute in his car. It was crazy, wonderful and unforgettable. We wake up and I get home in time to do what mommies do. Time to wake hubbie and kids up for school and work. Now that is how you start your day. O.K.

Chapter 8

Birthday Play

Today is June 23rd, My Birthday. I hear a knock on my door. It is my next-door neighbor. "Happy Birthday Bitch!" is what I hear when I open it. "What you doing today? Any plans?" I say, "Well, you already know my family and my husband don't have anything planned for me. I honestly don't know if they remember. You are the first one to tell me Happy Birthday. Anyway, Saint on his way to pick me for my Birthday Breakfast." She said, "Oh really." I reply, "Whatever bitch, yes really." He is taking me to get my chicken and eggs and raisin toast. I can already taste it." She said, "Alright, call me when you get back. And she heads back home. As she walks out my door, I see Saint's car pull up. I go out the door right behind her.

When I opened the passenger door, he has flowers, a card and a teddy bear on the seat for me. Happy Birthday Gorgeous One! And he kissed me like it is the first time he has ever kissed me. Soft but so powerful. Then he asks if I am hungry. I tell him I can eat. He replies, "Always." "Whatever Craig." Saint said, "Are we going smoke before or after we eat." We both say "both" at the same time. Saint say, Well, roll up Smokey." I say, "Give me the cigars Craig." And we bust out laughing. I roll up and we roll out to the restaurant. While we are eating, he asks if I have any plans for the rest of the day. I look up from my food kind of puzzled and say, "Yeah right, with who, Angel and King". He laughed and said, "Well, in that case can you be a big girl and stay out all night?" "Yeah, sure I can. I will tell my husband that I am going to my mom's house to help her unpack her boxes and get moved in. My brothers can baby sit for me since they live with me for free". I say, "What you got up your sleeve." "Don't worry about it just pack a play bag and be ready when I come pick you up." We finish eating, he dropped me back off at home and says he will call me when he is on the way to get me.

By 5p.m. my mom has already picked me up and I am at her house waiting for my call. "You're my little secret", comes through my phone, and my nipples get hard. I smile and answer it, "Hello young man." "Hey Birthday Girl. What you doing?" "I am at my mom's house." "That's even better, ask her to drop you off." "Where, at your crib?" "Nope, I got us a hotel room to spend your birthday in. I want us to spend our first night together." "Oh really." "Yes really." "O.K. Look at you spoiling me again. Text me the address and the room number. See you in a few I am on the way."

Fifteen minutes later my mom drops me off at the room. Before I get out the car my mom says, "I am so happy for you. Enjoy yourself you deserve it. Call me when you are ready to get picked up or just get dropped off at my house, so I can take you home." "Ok mommy, I love you thanks." "You know mommy got you." As I close the car door, I see my baby come down the stairs to greet me and carry my bag. Why wouldn't, he is a gangster and a gentleman. He is behind me as we walk to the room and I can feel his eyes on my booty. When we step inside the room, I am SPEECHLESS. When I tell you my baby got us a room, not just any room. It is nice as hell. Oh My God I can't believe it. It has a big ass jacuzzi tub in the middle of the floor. He has the room decorated with black and red balloons and white and red rose petals. Candles are lit and a bottle of wine is on ice. He has already ordered our food and it has been delivered. We Love Food as much as we love each other. There is a half zip of Ellenwood's finest loud on the bed. I see he took the liberty to roll four and smoke one while he waited on me to arrive. I am still standing at the door stuck in shock. Tears running down my face I feel my baby wrap his arms around me from behind. He kisses my neck and growls softly in my ear like an animal. Then he kisses my ear and whispers, "Happy Birthday Gorgeous One. Do you like your surprise?" Still crying, I turn around and hug him back. I squeeze him as tight as I can. "Yes, Yes, Yes. I Love it, so much." Nobody has ever done anything like this for me before. Thank you, thank you, thank you." Oh my God, thank you so much." He says, "You are so welcome baby."

After we eat our dinner. I get in the jacuzzi full of rose petal and bubbles. Bae hands me a glass of wine and a perfectly rolled blunt. He washes me and we smoke after the blunt is done he gets in with me I wash him. We get out and dry each other off. He massages me with lavender lotion. I fall asleep after the first ten minutes. This big bed is so soft, and I am so tired. He keeps massaging my whole body as I sleep. Of course, he let's me sleep because he knows how bad I need rest. I am in heaven. Saint Villo take me away!!! What more can a girl ask for? Best Sleep Ever!!! To get woke up the BEST FACE EVER!!!

Oh Yeah!!! His whole entire face is in my pie ya'll. I mean his face is buried between my thighs and his tongue is licking the inside part. As I begin to tremble and shake, I can feel myself cumming so much that it is dripping down the crack of my booty. He pulled himself up from my kitty, kissing my stomach and breast on the way up. He slides straight into me with now problem this time. Like a butcher's knife cutting through fresh hot pound cake. I don't think I have ever blacked out before… but BITCH!!!. I left this world. I know that for sure. We did it again and again until the sun came up. Other than during my massage, I did not sleep at all at this sleepover. ALL I CAN SAY IS BEST BIRTHDAY EVER!!!

Chapter 9

Anything and Everything Play

We are doing anything and everything together, so we build a company and name it just that. We are so ambitious and driven. We feed each other's egos so we feel like we can do anything that we want to do. Why not. Fuck It. I mean we are catering, massaging, open mics construction work, plus much more on top of entertainment and or addictions to each other. Now guess what. We are live on internet radio with our own show called Anything and Everything. We are talking to people and playing music two hours every Thursday from 8 p.m. to 10 p.m. We get to play Saint Villo DeVille music as much as we want. I get to say my poems and read my naughty stories on the air. We crack jokes and crack on each other the whole show. We are so funny together. I love seeing him smile and laugh. He's too serious most of the time. When we are live on the air, he opens up more. I see how much he needs me. He enjoys his life better when I am with him. The station is doing a big party for the employees. It is a 24-hour, yacht party on Lake Lanier. The two of us are going to do massages as one of the vendors for the VIPs. After setting up our equipment on the top level we go downstairs to the main level where everyone is too smoke.

When we walk out, we hear a guy talking to everyone. We are not really listening at first. Then he turns his attention to us, all of a sudden. He says, "How long have you two been married?" We look at each other and back at him. Then we both say, "We not married we just friends, at the same damn time. Suspect or nawl? He said, No, seriously stop playing. How long have ya'll been married?" We both say, "We are for real, we not married. Saint said, "She has a husband. He dropped her off here." The reader says, "Well, I can feel ya'll connection, the energy is insane. That's why the fish are going crazy in the water and the waves in the lake keep rocking the yacht."

Saint keeps staring at me the whole time that the medium is talking about us. Everyone is out there listening closely to what he has to say. The other people out there are all deep into this type of reading stuff. We are the newbies. He tells us that we were married before in a previous life. The more he talks about us the hotter I become. I feel like a volcano about to erupt. Some invisible force has taken control of me.

My body is locked in the chair that I am sitting in and I am trembling and shaking out of control. Everyone stares at me in awe as Saint sits two feet away from me and gives me a 30- minute orgasm without even touching me. The medium Black says, to Saint, "You know you are doing this to her, don't you?" Saint replies, "How am I doing it she is not even near me." "The power that you two share is magnificent. She is your true soulmate, your ancient spiritual wife." After about an hour of me loosing my mind in front of everyone, Saint grabs me consoles me and wipes my tears away. He kisses my forehead like only he can do. It makes me settle down enough to allow me to stand on my shaky legs. He hugs me and whispers in my ear, "Come on hot girl, Mr. Daddy got something to satisfy your passion." We walk pass everybody and go to our cabin. We don't even say one word to each other. We undress each other and make the most sweet, slow and passionate love that I have ever come to know in my life. Until we fall fast asleep.

Chapter 10

Water Play

The next day we wake up, and hell yeah, the rabbits are back at it again. Two, three, maybe four times I can't remember. Can you tell we missed each other? It has been a few days, almost a week since we have been alone. Just work, work, work work… You would think it has been months or a year the way we are going at it. It is getting too hot and this room is too small. The sheets are drenched from our sweat and my cum.

Bae said, "Let's go take a shower and get cleaned up. So, we go get in the shower. We start washing each other. Soon his member is in my hand covered in soap and I am stroking it up and down as I moan in his ear. He asks, "Are you cumming already, girl?" "Hush boy." He tells me, "Who you think you talking too? I am your master watch your mouth." He turns me around facing the shower wall and he grabs my neck and bends me over from behind. He jams his hard, fat soapy rod deep into me with one push.

People are already in the kitchen. We know, but we give NO fucks. It is getting so good; I can't keep quite anymore. I start screaming and moaning loud as I cum, back to back to back. My baby covers my mouth with his hand. "SSHH everybody is going to hear you." I say, "I don't care (tooting my lips up at him) give it to me." I started sucking on his fingers as he drills me. Harder and harder deeper and deeper and I get louder and louder. When he cums, he gets just as loud as me. So, we have used up all the hot water, so it's time for us to get out. As we close the door and head back down to our cabin, I hear someone yell from the kitchen, 'Boy, ya'll don't play." We both start laughing. I say, "Oops you think they heard us?"

Chapter 11

Party Play

Well as you can guess by now, we can't get enough. Even when we think we had enough we need more. Its about that time. I get fresh waiting for my baby so we can step out and hit the scene. His aunt is having her 60th birthday flashback party. We show up and as usual all eyes are on us. Saint introduces me to everyone at the party. We fix our plate and sit down at a table with his parents. The music is loud. We watched his family on the dance floor while we ate. His mom stood up and went to do the electric slide with her sisters. His mom and aunts are too turned up. They are so freaking adorable. I love me some them. I finish my plate and look over at my baby. He is staring at me and biting his bottom lip. He knows I can't resist him when he does that. I lean over and tell him I am ready to smoke now. We sneak through the crowd unnoticed while they are all partying. His car is on the dark side of the parking lot. We have a little bit of privacy, I guess...

He opens my door and I get in the car. The blunts are already rolled so I grab one and light it up as he walks around to his door. I take a long deep pull. It rushes to my head." Ooohh wee that's good." He got in and said, "Oh you like that Ellenwood gas huh?" "Yes, indeed I do." We are dressed so fly and looking so good we can't keep our hands off each other. While he is smoking, I unzip his pants so I can play with my best friend. As soon as it pops out his pants, I say, hello and kiss it softly and begin to lick it up and down. I was sucking just the head at first very gentle and sweet. Then I went deeper and sucked a little harder and harder. He kept getting harder and harder in my mouth. I could feel it throbbing in my throat. It is making me so wet. I lifted myself up off the seat enough to take my panties off under my dress. Then I mounted him and rode him in the driver seat. He squeezed my booty cheeks with both hands and lifted me up and down while e was licking and suck my nipples driving me insane.

He just bought me this dress yesterday and it is balled up around my waist getting sweaty. Tragic... The windows are fogged up. I am screaming and yelling. My fingers are gripping the head rest. His hands are controlling my hips as he makes circles inside of me. WOW, he is full of surprises. We continue like this for a while and then move to the back seat to get more comfortable. I lay down and he gets on top of me. I try to wrap my legs around him. He grabs my ankles and puts my legs on his shoulders. He bawls me up completely until my feet touch the ceiling. He is tearing my red ass up. Oh my God, oh my God, it hurts so bad. It gets so big every time I suck it, WTF… Saint says to me, "You like when I hurt this pussy don't you." I say, "You know I do, you know I do." He starts sucking my nipples again. Then I squirt all over him. He came at the exact same time. It was explosive. We dried ourselves off, got redressed, smoked another one and eased our way back in. We made a quick stop on the dance floor in route to the drinks. Yep, we thirsty as hell. Serious cotton mouth. Later, the party wines down and people are leaving. We say our goodbyes and head back to Covington.

He drops me off at home. I walk in the house still buzzing. It is pitch black dark in here. I hear a voice in the room. "Red." I'm like WTF am I tripping. "Red". I hear it again. Damn, I'm hearing shit. Then the light comes on. It is my husband. He said, "We need to talk, sit down." I say, "What's up." He replies with the saddest look on his face as if he lost his best friend. "I have lost you. I am losing my family." "Boy, what are you talking about?" I'm drunk a hell. Again, he said, "I lost you." "Why you say that?" I ask him. He replies, "I have never seen you glow like this before. You are so happy. I have never seen you so happy before. I know you love me, but you are in love with him. I also know that you are a one-man kind of girl. Once you start sleeping with him…. It's a wrap for me." I told him, "All I can say is I am glad you know." After that we were both sat silent for a long while. I simply stood up and went to lay down with my babies and dream about Mr. Daddy. LOL.

Chapter 12

Ferris Wheel Play

I have lived in the Atlanta area for many years now. Saint V was born here. Neither one of us has never been to the ferries wheel before. I told Saint that I wanted to go there and one day he surprised me, out of nowhere. It was just a normal day for us hitting the block serving customers. Smoking and eating good. Next thing I know my baby said, "Guess what I got a surprise for you." "What is it, tell me." We are almost there wait and see." And wouldn't you know it just like that we were pulling up at the ferris wheel downtown. "Are you freaking serious right now. Bae for real don't play. We are really finna get on there?" He said, "Damn Right. You told me you wanted to ride it." That is Saint V. for ya. Always making my dreams come true. No matter how big or small. Anything I ask for, he makes it happen. We are smoking when we pull up and we burn one more before we go get in line. While my baby is paying, I got my back to him looking at the ferris wheel. I am super excited.

When I turn around my baby hands me a box of chocolates and 1 single rose. "For you pretty lady." "Why thank you young man", I reply and give him a kiss. The line is moving fast. We are next. We are the only two people in our compartment. This so romantic. The wheel starts to turn as more people get on. We start kissing as our compartment keeps rising higher until we are at the top. Atlanta looks so freaking beautiful from up here. If you have never been on the ferris wheel in Atlanta, then it is a must for your bucket list. It is dark outside, so the city lights are shining like the stars above us. I am sitting on my baby lap now and kissing him while he rubs between my legs. He whispers in my ear, "Now you see why I told you to where a dress. After I am hot and ready, he pulls his hard dick out and slide it right pass my thong into my wet wabbit." All the way in. I sit down and grind as the wheel rotates. I think the other people can see us but who cares. We have our lights off and the radio and air on. That is enough privacy for us to do what we do best. I opened my eyes in the middle of an orgasm just in time to realize that the ride is about to stop. So, do I stop? NO, I go faster and faster until I make us cum. Literally, as the door opens, I am getting off of him. We get out and while we walk to the car it feels like he is still in me and I feel our cum running down my inner thighs. Man, what a ride!!!....

Chapter 13

Crazy for the Dick Play

It's official. I am obsessed. And I love it. I can not and will not be without them. My man nor my dick. I have to have them; it is a must. It is to the point where I get extremely pissed if I can't get them when I want them. I need to have them. Look at it from my point of view. Yes, I am married. Yes, he has a girl. I am releasing ten years of sexual frustration, loneliness, anger, and so much more. There is nothing anyone can say or do at this point. As time passes the drama starts and we began to have arguments like every other couple on earth. Now we are fussing and fighting. My baby is mad at me because I keep pressuring him to move out. I don't want him living with her. I always want to have access to him.

Saint decided to move into an extended stay hotel room to save up his money and shut me the fuck up. I'm just being honest. I am so fucking happy. My baby is on the way to come get me so we can go to his room. Like always my baby got us some loud to go with my mid. He tells me to make myself at home and he goes to the ice machine. He takes the key and locks me in. He is always so protective of me. I take this time to get in the tub and soak my tired body. My phone is playing music so I don't know he is back in the room until he opens the bathroom door and gives me a lit blunt. He is smoking one two. We toast our blunts like champagne glasses and he leaves me to my bath. I never get to bathe and relax like this at home. This is SO freaking peaceful. Saint sticks his head back in the door and says, "I am about to cook dinner for you so take your time." "Are you serious?" "Yes, baby I am serious." With tears in my eyes, "Nobody ever cooks for me. I cook for everybody all day every day." Why am I such a cry baby when I am around him, I don't know. I am Thug Barbie. Thugs don't cry. What is wrong with me?

Still sitting in the tub 15 minutes later crying thinking to myself. I smell the food and It smells amazing. I yell through the door, "Baby!" Saint opens the door and walks in "Yes, baby." He notices that I'm crying and immediatly holds my face in both of his hands. "What's the matter sexy?" I say, "I need to tell you something that I have wanted to say for a while. I love you and I am falling more and more everyday please tell me I am not alone." My baby replies, "I love you girl. You know that though don't you." I said, "Yes, I know. I guess I just needed to hear you say it. People have said it to me before, but you are the first person to treat me like they love me. You show me every day and I appreciate everything we do together. That's why I had to say it and hear it from you. And I know you need to hear it as well. Saint says, "Its O.K. we both have experienced fake love before. Now we get to experience real love together with each other. Now come on let's eat fat girl." "Whatever fat boy." My baby helps me out the tub and dries me off.

    I got straight in the bed under the covers because I was cold. Saint bring my plate to the bed. He serves me his famous spaghetti with garlic cheese bread. Baby this shit look so fucking good smiling from ear to ear. I lift the plate to my nose and inhale the aroma. Yummy…. I take my first bite I look up smile at him and stare at him as I chew and swallow. "Oh My God, Baby, when I tell you this shit so GOT DAMN GOOD…" "I am so glad you like it." he replies. I say, "No, I don't like it, I love it." My baby grabs him a plate. We eat while we watch a movie. After we are done, I take both plates to the sink. I clean them and lay back in the bed cuddling up to my big chocolate teddy bear. He is running his fingers through my hair and massaging my scalp. He kisses my forehead and ears and neck so softly. While he is massaging my scalp I and massaging my best friend. As I ease my head under the cover and begin to suck him off, about two minutes in he pulls me up and tells me to sit on his face and suck it. I put him back in my mouth and turn my kitty to his face. Bull's eye! Straight on his tongue. He slides it straight in me and I cum instantly. So after two hour of that good nasty 69. He falls inside of me and keeps hunching the HELL out of me for two more hours until we both pass out.

Chapter 14

Back and Forth Play

If you can't guess by now me and Saint are now an item. My husband I are officially separated but still living under the same roof. Crazy I know right? I have two small children, King and Angel who are in school so I can't just up and move them. I am trying my best to make this situation work. I am going back and forth Monday through Friday. I am staying at the room with my baby every night and getting dropped off at my husband house every morning to get my kids off to school. After my kids come home, I feed them bathe them and put them to sleep before Bae comes to pick me up every night. Now the tables have turned. We are yelling at each other every day. My baby wants me to move completely out of my house and bring my babies with me to live with him. So of course, I go. Everything is going great for the first two weeks. Then my psycho started to kick in. My mind was playing tricks on me. I began to question why is he with me why does he want me? I don't have any thing to give him. I have two special needs babies. Plus, I am married already. What am I doing? Is he crazy? We have a fight about something, and I move back to my husband house. I could not eat, sleep, barely breathe for the three days I was there. I was so lovesick. I move back to the room with Saint, but I left my kids with there with their dad. When we make it inside the room, I ask my baby if we can find a house to move to. I say, "This room is too small for me, you and my babies. I refuse to be without you, and you know I can't be without King and Angel."

I am nervous to hear his response. How will he react? He says, "Alright, bet. Then he picked me up and tossed me on the bed and said, "Now give me my pussy." Then he jumped my bones. I stopped counting my orgasms after number 7. It's a good thing he had two beds in there we soaked one of them so bad we could not sleep in it.

Chapter 15

Daylight Play

So, we are riding out hitting the block. And just like that BAM it hits me. I am hot and bothered. What's new? "Bae, I need some" He replies, "Right now?" I just look down at his lap. "That's my baby", he says. The salon that he used to rent a room at has relocated. So, we pull up in the parking lot since it is empty. Yeah, it is broad day light and we are on Flat Shoals Parkway with traffic passing by. This was the closest place we could find with my hot ass. No time to waste we are straight at it again. With my ass in the air and my face in the back seat. My baby standing up in that thang digging deep and so good. He flipped me over, and with no hesitation back to pounding and drilling away. This shit is so amazing each time is better than the time before it. I have never heard of nothing like this in my life. We have the door open just a little to let in some air. But with every pump I am being pushed against the door and it is opening more and more. So, with my head hanging out the car damn near touching the ground, we keep going at it. Not once did we stop until he came twice. I came God knows how many times. We are so wild.

Chapter 16

We Got It Bad Play

We got it bad. Let me tell you just how bad. On October 27, 2019, in the middle of writing this book, as a matter of fact. While my baby is typing for me since I refuse, because I am a spoiled brat, this happened. I am sitting next to him just watching him type. He is so intense when he is focused. I love to see him in action no matter what type of work he is doing. I can never keep my hands to myself when I get close to him. I am just feeling and touching away. My baby is so focused he is not paying me any mind. So, I put my hand in his pants and pulled it out. I started licking and slurping and sucking until it started growing hard in my mouth. He was stuck in a trance.

I popped him out of my mouth with a loud sucking noise and I say, "Are you ready for a break now? "Yes, it is definitely break time." He says to me as he follows me to our bedroom. Our clothes fall to the floor as soon as the door closes. We are standing in front of the mirror completely naked hugging kissing and moaning. I tell him thank you so much for typing my book. I really appreciate you more than words can express. He squeezes my booty and says, "You know Mr. Daddy got you girl." "Yeah, I know now let me show you my appreciation. Lay on the bed Mr. Daddy." "I want to give you a massage for a change. He said, "Good my lower back is so stiff." I lotion him up and start making small circles with my knuckles on the hard muscles of his back. He is breathing deep and moaning as his muscles relax. After he is feeling better I roll him over so he is face up. I start massaging his manhood with my tongue. Then I slide him all the way down my throat. As he pushes my head down holding me there and making me gag.   Now I am dripping wet cumming from sucking him off. Sucking my baby dick turns me on so fucking much. Just to watch how much he enjoys it give me pleasure. I hop up and jump straight on my dick. Bouncing up and down nice and slow while he grips my booty cheeks. He gives them a little smack. "Whose pussy is this?" He says. "Yours Mr. Daddy every inch of me belongs to you." You own me Baby. Now make me feel like you do." He keeps slapping my ass repeatedly and stroking in and out of me, as I hold my hips up high and pop that coochie. I hear the sound of my wetness squishing. It sounds like my pussy is talking. Why is the sound and the smell of my pussy turning me on even more? We have been together for four years now. It is getting even better. And here I go again cumming back to back. Sweat is pouring off of my baby's face. So, I hop of the dick and turn on the fan. I suck him until he is extra hard again and slide right back down on it. And I ride till I can't no more. We both cum at the same time. The kids are going wild at our door as soon as we roll out the bed. Perfect timing. We get dressed and head out the room. We got to finish this good ass book for ya'll. So back to typing.

Chapter 17

Storage Play

It's getting close to time for us to move in our very own house together. Can you believe it? I know right, me either. I am so so, so freaking excited. I can't wait. This is going to be so perfect, is all I keep thinking to myself the whole time we are riding. We get us a bite to eat a bag and head to the storage unit to get our stuff to take it home. WOW, Home! That sounds so dam nice. We burned the U-haul down on the way there. We pull up at the storage unit. He hired some help that was supposed to meet us here but they not here yet. We get out and head inside the unit. First, we set the small stuff outside to get the bigger things in first. Then this way we will be able to get the smaller things on top. It is summertime in Georgia and it's too fucking hot!! So, we both are coming out of clothes. No shirt gang as we still load the truck. He has on a pair of basketball shorts. I got on my sports bra and some tight shorts. I stand inside the door of the storage unit waiting for my baby to walk in.

As soon as he gets close to me, I grab that big dick and ask him, "Do you know what I need now?" He gives me a sexy look then pushes me up against the wall kissing me and tonguing me down like never before. "Turn around a bend over this chair like a good little girl." Mr. Daddy says to me. "Ok, Mr. Daddy", I reply back. He pulls my shorts and thong down to my ankles and begin to have his way with me. I can already feel myself cumming before he even gets it in. I want him so bad. We are going straight ham in this storage unit.

Now has picked me up and he is pushing that big powerful dick up inside me deeper and deeper making tears flow from my eyes. I stutter as I try to get the words out. "You're hurting me baby, baby, baby you are hurting me so fucking bad. Mr. Daddy says back to me. "I know, I love to hurt my tight, sweet, fat pussy. You love when Mr. Daddy hurt that pussy too. Don't you love when Mr. Daddy hurt that pussy?" "Yes, Mr. Daddy I love when you hurt your little tight pussy. "YES, YES, YES." I yell out and I cumming so hard at the same time. We can here a truck pulling up. The help is finally here. Time to finish packing and go HOME, SWEET!

Chapter 18

New Home Play

We make it back to the house after four trips of taking things to the house from the storage. Since our helped lived in Covington, we paid them and took the last load to Atlanta ourselves. But, the very first load we took to the house was a treat. Let me tell you. When we are on the way there it starts to rain on us. The helpers pull over under some shelter and wait for the rain to stop because we have our stuff on the back of the pickup truck. We are so lit right now. My baby takes a deep breath and says to me, "We gone keep pushing since we are almost there." I said "Really." He said, "Yep, like 10 more minutes and we will be at our new house baby. Can you believe it?" "No, I can't. I am just so happy and overjoyed right now. It's like you always just keep finding ways to make my dreams come true." I said to him, smiling from ear to ear. Saint grabs my hand and kisses it. "I can't wait for you to see it baby. I bet you like it." We get off the express way at Jonesboro Rd exit and shortly, we pull up to a ranch style, brick cottage house. It is so beautiful. The yard is huge and there is a rosebush right next to my front door.

My baby hands me the keys and says," Didn't I tell you I would get you a house." "Yes, Yes, you did baby. Thanks, my God." I say back to him and give him a kiss and hugging and squeezing him tight as I can. He tells me, "Open the door baby." I unlock the door, turn the knob and walk in. There are hardwood floor that look like new. A blue countertop that is in the kitchen beside the living room. I will be able to see my T.V. and watch my babies, while I work in my beautiful kitchen. It's so perfect for me, I love it. We walk around and my baby shows me the house and believe it or not we get to it again, right there in the empty house. I know you all are like there is no way we just did it. Wrong. I still owe him another nut from the storage play. I got mine a few times. I stay ready all day every day and my baby don't mind giving it to me all day every day.

He wants it as bad as I do right now. He keeps teasing me, rubbing my booty and kittycat as he introduces me to my new house. "This is the laundry room" rub, rub. "This is the master bedroom" rub, rub. "This will be my office, the kid's rooms, the bathrooms, ect… rub, rub, rub, rub. I mean I have a visible wet spot in my shorts by now. I head back to the kitchen and he follows right behind me. I want to try out that pretty blue countertop. It is raining outside but it is still hot. That countertop felt so cool on my skin. I leaned over it and grabbed the edge. I got to hold on tight for this. I am waiting for him to slide into me because he has been hard for the last five minutes. But I feel him lips on my butt checks instead. I get so weak in the knees. All I hear I get so weak in the knees by Xscape in my head. He pecks my left cheek and slaps my right one. Then he slaps my left cheek and pecks my right one. Then he licks my spine slowly with his tongue pressed into my back. Now I feel his fat head press against my outer lips. He pumps one quick time to pop inside of me. My wetness coats the tip of his hardness. He pulls back out and rubs his wet head in circles on my clit. I am trembling as he goes back in, all the way this time.

A clear puddle is forming beneath me, on my flawless hardwood floor, in between my legs. All I hear is my ass clapping and cum squirts splashing to the floor. The thunder crashes and he started to speed up. The faster he went the louder I yelled. The thunder hit again. He slapped my booty and palmed it like a basketball. He slowed down his pace to a slow nasty grind. This nigga is the butt naked truth! He is holding back on me so he can last longer in this good wet wabbit. I love him so much. I have never been so completely satisfied like this. His fingers are sliding down my sides and waist as he rocks me back and forth. As he grabs me and releases me, his pumps bounce me in a rhythm. I hear my voice, but I don't know what I am saying. He is grunting and growling like a beast behind me. My orgasms won't stop. I mean back to back to back. He keeps getting larger harder and harder in my tight putty tat until, Bam!!!! He shoots his thick hot cum inside of me. Without any warning at all, his hot milk hits the back wall of my cookie. He keeps bouncing me at the same slow, nasty pace as he fills me up. He stays in me still hard as he rests on my back, breathing on my neck and ear. We separate our bodies after we catch our breath. As we put our clothes on, we notice that the rain has stopped, and the sun is starting to come out. We look at each other and we both begin to laugh.

We are both thinking about what the reader told us at the yatch party. Then my baby says, "Come on Nasty, let's get moved in."

Chapter 19

Fantasy Play

With things taking off, events are keeping us busy. We have been doing so many comedy -shows, open mics, radio personalities, and parades. You name it, we do it. We also miss a lot of opportunities because we have no help with the babies. So, we decide to let my two older brothers come move in to be our help for a while. Once they move in, things really got sweet. We can finally get away alone and fulfill some of my fantasies. A movie comes out that I want to see, and I ask Mr. Daddy to take me on a drive-in movie date. "Yes, Gorgeous One," is his response.

So, I am getting dressed for my date, and my baby phone gets a text message. I read it and call him into the room. I say, "You just got a text about performing tonight. What's good Craig? We already dressed and going out. Saint Villo Deville might as well go give the people a show." There a lot of couples that smoke a lot, but I bet we are the only couple in the world who call each other that on a constant basis as pet names. I call him Craig more than I call him Bae now. SO His reply is, "You already know Smokey. We can do that before we hit the movie. You not ready yet? I'm about to clean my tools out the car and put in our performance stuff." I turn back to face the mirror as I say, "Ok Baby, I am right behind you."

As I walk out into the living room, I hear my baby wrestling with King and talking to my brothers. I tell them, "Ya'll need to stop before you mess up your clothes. Damn you fine boy." "Why thank you, sexy lady and you are as stunning as ever.". I say, "Are you sure this is not doing to much, I feel overdressed." Saint says, "You are perfect." My brother Mike says, "Ya'll some super stars, you supposed to be dressed like that. Looking like Da Hood Bonnie and Clyde". King is slapping my baby in his back, but he is so zoned out looking at me he doesn't even react to it. Mike says, "Let me take a picture of ya'll." He really is a fan and good family. We appreciate his support too. I grab Bae hand and pull him up off the couch as he passes the blunt to my other brother Sleepy and poses for our picture. Now, Picture it.... I am in a tight fitting, cream, off the shoulder gown. The bottom half is shear up to my thighs. The tops of my perky girls are barely noticeable. Classy and sassy the same time. My gold cowgirl boots underneath. Gold jewelry and accessories. Gold glasses with no lenses in them. (Yeah, I started that… You're welcome). Saint Villo Deville is in OG mode. He is sharp as hell in his black Bossalino, black and gold shades, cream button down, with gold cufflinks, gold and diamond earrings, brown cream and tan scarf with matching neck tie, tailored dark brown slacks, pressed and creased with black and gold shoes, matching my fly. Cuz that's just how we do.

Mike took some pictures and we posted them on IG and FB. We make sure the babies are squared away and me and my boo are out this bit. We leave the house and head downtown. We hit the stage at 10:30 p.m. and we kill the show as always. We gave them music and comedy. The crowd is recording and taking pics of us and singing the hooks to our songs. We eat us some wings, shrimp and fries then we pack up our gear and head out the door. Some of the people walked us out to the car to tell us how much they enjoyed us and to get our contact information. We told them to go to YouTube and search for Saint Villo DeVille to see our concert footage and stand-up comedy and subscribe to the channel. They even took pictures with us and followed our social media pages before we left. They told us how good our business cards looked. I said "My baby designed these cards. Give us a call if you need anything designed and printed."

We roll up, light up and roll out to Moreland, to hit the drive in. After we pay and get parked, we open the wine, sip and smoke some more before the movie starts. The tea we drunk with dinner plus the wine is too much for my bladder. I ask my baby which way is the bathroom. He says, "It is on the side of the concession stand". I say, "I will be right back I got to use it." Saint looks me and start laughing. I say, "What Craig? He says, "That sweet pussy hot already." Then his smile turns into a poker face and he says, "You still ain't going nowhere by yourself. I will walk with you. People snatch folks in the public now days. I know somebody is gonna want to snatch up your fine ass." I obey, sit still and wait for him to walk around and open my door.

He helps me out and holds my hand as I wobble on my heels and say to him, "O.K. mister." (In my Color Purple, Ceily voice) "M-I-S-T-E-R. I gotta go to school." "Smokey bring your silly ass on here." Is his response. He holds be my butt cheek to keep me balanced as I lean on him and walk. He is waiting right outside the women's bathroom door for me when I come out. We kiss and back to the car. Bladder empty, check, belly full, check, geeked out my mind check. Wet and ready, check. It looks like the movie is about to start. Now ask me which movie we went see. I don't know. I guess I should say my movie is about to start. To this day I can't remember what was on that big ass screen. I think, maybe it was all that big dick blocking my view. Let me tell ya 'bout it.

So, I can feel him in the back of my throat throbbing and getting harder with each suck, I can feel his fingers pulling my panties down under my skirt. He pulls them all the way off me while I bend over his lap with my knees in the back seat and my booty in the air. I don't stop sucking as he begins to finger my putty tat with three fingers. I can feel the cream sliding out of me as he massages my insides. He lays me on top of him as we 69. He licks my clit and lips so slow and soft I can barely take it. I keep trying to lift up off of his hot tongue. He keeps pulling me back down on his mouth by my booty cheeks. He is holding on for dear life and slurping my entire pie with each stroke. I can't get away. Finally, I hear the words that I am yearning for. He stops eating me and says, "Give Mr. Daddy my fat pussy. It's time to complete this fantasy of yours." My baby just keeps making love to me in all types of positions.

He has no shame at all. He has the car rocking side to side like we hitting switches in a 64. He tells me to ride him backward. I don't even think. I Just do it. I am doing the reverse cowgirl like a real live porn star. This angle is putting him in brand new places that have never been touched before. My hips go into auto pilot. I grab both head rests and pull myself and drop myself down repeatedly as he poked my back wall. We hear music playing at the end of the movie. That is when he grabs my waist and starts picking me up and pulling me back down on him hard and fast. He is ready to give me my protein. Filler up Big Boy. He me pulls up to the tip and holds the head up against my lips. He skeets his white gravy in me. It gushes out onto my clit and my lips. He pokes it back in and keeps skeeting more inside of me. My baby kept fucking me as white whip creamed started to foam up around his thick man meat. I kept on going. Slowly rocking back and forth with him inside of me. He was spreading my booty cheeks and blowing on my booty hole, until we notice cars cranking up and leaving. I turn to Bae and say, "Does this mean the movie over." He replies, "I am afraid so my little nasty girl, … until we get home."

Chapter 20

Driveway Play

Have you ever had one of those day when wanted to get away but did not want to go away? We figured out a way to do just that. Instead of spending gas money, paying for parking and cover charge to party with strangers. We made a place with free entry no dress code and smoke all you want. Try this. Get fly get in the car, turn the music up, and keep that bitch in park cause we ain't going nowhere. What? Now it is time to turn up. Pop that first bottle, cause now we got bottles instead of drinks. Smoke and don't pass that shit. Its your party you can do what you want to do. Let's get naked, hell why not. Remember now, this is my driveway play not yours. S0 you don't have to get naked unless you want to. But I do.

As my baby undresses me with his eyes. He is gently pinching my nipples through my shirt and kissing the side of my face and down my neck. This is driving me fucking crazy in the best way. He put his hand under my shirt and cups my bare breast. He is lifting my shirt exposing them. And he says, "Peek-a- boo I see you" and give each of them a kiss. Now he is nibbling and sucking my left nipple tasting my breast milk, as always. They say milk do a body good. And man, I do love his body. I must say. Still, even now, when I look at him, he continues to take my breath away. My baby is about to burst out of his pants. He is so freaking hard, I mean stiff, firm as a rock. I want to suck it so damn bad; I feel drool leaking from the corner of my mouth. YES! I love to suck my master's big dick. The way it fills my mouth and throat really turns me on. All I can do is suck on it, cum and moan. I suck it until my jaws get soar.

Then I say, "Now take this pussy. Its yours. Hit it from the back, slap my ass. You know I like that." With no hesitation he did exactly what I said. Our back seats lay flat, so we have as much room as we need in here. He gets behind me and slides his hard head up and down my outer lips making me squirt uncontrollably. Then he sticks it and gives me all of it. I promise you I can feel ever single bit of him. Really, I do have tears forming in my eyes and I tell him I love you and he says it back over and over. The more he says he loves me the more he makes my little tight pussy cum. Pushing me all the way down putting it deeper inside me until I say, "Please daddy I can't take no more." Then pulling me up while he is stays inside of me, I begin to bounce on it. And boy did I bounce on it like I never bounced before. I am going to make sure that I am the last woman that will ever get this good dick. All those years of sexual frustration are in the past. I have met the man of my dreams and he his turning me out, constantly. He is a super-freak, but he has met his match. I can't believe his exes let him go. Thank You Bitches…

Chapter 21

Storm Play

One Friday me and my baby were at home watching our show footage, as we post stuff and make notes on what changes we will make. My phone rings, it's my mom. She is panicking about a storm that is supposed to be hitting Atlanta. She is afraid our house will be flooded, or our power will go out or something. After going back and forth with her on the phone about us driving all the way to Conyers to her house, I finally say, "O.K. mommy you win. I am about to get the kids dressed and head out there." First, I must pack the survival kit. Babies, pullups, wipes, toys, clothes, snacks, movies, DVD player, bud, cigarillos, lighters. And we out dis bit….

Angel and King fall asleep on the way to Conyers. When we pull into my mom's yard, I am greeted by my niece, Lani. She runs out of the front door, on her little 3-year-old legs. "Matta Head," she screams with her arms out wide. I scream, "Matta Head" and grab her in a tight hug, as she jumps in my arms. She missed me and I missed her. My mom and my sister stand at the door looking ugly in the face, because my niece is so obsessed with me. She thinks I am the greatest. It doesn't matter how long it has been since we have seen each other. It doesn't matter where we are at. It is the same greeting and reaction each and every time.

We get the babies and the luggage and survival kit in the house. We give Angel and King their snacks and they go play with their cousin. We chill in the house with my sisters and brothers for a few hours. We are burning it down and watching movies. Eerbody rolling up. We got dis bit smoked out. My mom walks out of her bedroom and the smoke chokes her as she walks down the hall. "Ya'll ain't nothing but a bunch of junkies!" She says between coughs. We all bust out laughing. And she goes back into her room shaking her head. "Don't make no damn sense", is the last thing we all hear before she closes her door. Time passes, everybody is geeked, zoned out, stuck in the movie except for little ole me. I lean over and whisper in my baby ear. I say, "She is throbbing. You know what that means." He looks at me, I nod at his lap and then I nod towards the door. We both get up and walk outside without anybody even noticing. We get into the back seat of our car, that is parked in my mom's driveway. Fuck it, why not? The kids are good. It's dark outside. I'm, high, hot and ready. Let the fun begin.

We start kissing like some high school kids. For about 10 minutes we are licking and sucking each other tongues. He knows that his kiss is what got my ass and he still makes me so horny when he does me like this. His hands are all over me touching, rubbing and squeezing every inch of me. I am so hot I am about to explode. I can't take it no more. So, I rip it out of his pants and start sucking it, while I am pulling off my panties. A soon as he is rock hard, I waste no time I jump right on him, cumming instantly.

My baby said, "Damn girl, you cumming already", as he pulls me close, pushing deeper in me. He is moaning slow grinding all in my juicy pussy. Do ya'll know what I am talking about? I am facing him, his mouth is all over my breasts. His tongue is teasing my stiff nipples. I hear squishy noises coming from under me. "Oh my God girl I feel your cum running down my balls." The next thing I know I hear my mom yelling my name from the front door. Do I stop? Hell NO! I lean over still on the dick and open the car door. I yell back, "What Ma?" "Can you cook?" "Yeah, Ma." I hear the door close, and I go back at it. I have no clue if she knew what we were doing since she never walked out there. Or did she? Both of us are sweating bad but we not about to stop no time soon. An hour later, we go back inside, and I cook.

Chapter 22

Dress Up Play

New place, new start, new things, new hair, new nails, new clothes, new pole. Yep, that's right. I got me a pole!!! My baby already put it up for me. I love me some him. I am dancing around it, super excited, I can't wait to try it. We are trying all kinds of new things. Dressing up and role playing on top of acts of affection in public places. We start to include toys and food to our foreplay. One night, I dress up in my white Goddess outfit for him. When he comes home from work I tell him, "Get in the tub and soak then meet me in the bedroom." When he walks in and sees me laying there in all white he says, "I have an Angel in my bed. There is a God." I say, "You are my God." Then he says, "And you are my Goddess."

He climbs on the bed and we start face fucking. That is the sideways 69, if ya'll don't know. (You're welcome for saving your neck). After about 30 minutes later, he was on top of me, deep inside me, as I laid on my back. He was looking me straight in my eyes and going ham with a nasty grin on his face growling like a wild beast. Out of nowhere, he grabs my neck and squeezes my throat with his right hand. I am stunned at first, but I do not stop him. I don't know why. This shit is really turning me on, to give him total control and allow him to have his way with Mr. Daddy's nasty little girl. My baby is such a damn freak! I love him so much.

The way he makes me feel is unexplainable. My mind, my body, and my soul; he has total control. I love the fact that when he is inside of me, he makes me feel a though he owns me. And every inch of me belongs to him. He says off the wall stuff like I am his property and it makes my emotions go bonkers. I feel protected and valued and appreciated and dominated all at the same time. He is expressing his need for me in his life. He is bonded to me and I am bonded to him. Every time he climaxes in me his hot man fluid sends his energy into every cell of my body. I feel bold I feel strong I feel powerful. He takes me to another world where nothing matters but me. For the first time ever in my whole life, it's just about me. I never want it to end and I know it never will. No, we are not perfect so don't get it twisted. We argue and fight just like real couples do. But we always pray and fuck every day. Make sure to say, "I love you." Because it goes a long way.

Chapter 23

23 is Us Play

Twenty-three is just one of our numbers, so we will focus on that one. Twenty-three is us. Both of our birthdays are on the 23rd of the month. We celebrate our love and our lives together every month on the 23rd. Yeah, that is right I said every month. So, it's like when it is his birthday, it is my birthday and when it is my birthday, it is his birthday. Crazy right, Crazy sweet!! After two years of doing this we still be excited and surprised every single time. Some how the day always sneaks up on us. I may wake my baby up with a kiss and say, "Happy Anniversary," or I will wait until we are in the shower together and get all up on him and whisper in it in his ear. Sometimes, I write him a love letter and pack it in his lunch that he takes to work. And when I tell you the look on his face or to receive the phone call, "Hey Gorgeous One, Happy Anniversary to you" It sends chills up my spine and keeps a smile on my face, that he knows is going to be there all day.

On this particular twenty-third, things were crazy bad, and it was crazy good. My life is wonderful my life is amazing my life is great I must say. Still like anyone else, my life can be and is hard, and I do mean hard. My life was much harder before I found the other half of me. Saint V. Like I mentioned that both of my babies are special needs. My son King has Autism. My daughter, Angel has ADHD and Emotional Disorder. I myself also was suffering with depression and suicidal thoughts. All I can say is that God is real, and he definitely loves me. This wonderful man of mine saved me more than once in so many ways; from my family from what I thought were friends, from my ex-husband, from my life, most of all from myself. I was killing and destroying me. I did not love me. I didn't know how. I was so used to loving and caring for everyone else. Loving everyone else was to love me, so I thought.

I have experienced things that I never though of doing since I met Saint Villo DeVille. His confidence and ego cause me to step my boss up. He gives me this pride and power to accomplish anything and everything. I gave him my heart and he gave me the world. In these four years we have performed all over Atlanta. We have ridden horses together and went on the ferris wheel ride. (I know ya'll didn't forget that.) He has wined and dined me, and we even took a romantic horse drawn carriage ride downtown. We have our own house together and we love being at home together. I can write another book about the places that we have been and the things we have done. So yeah, you get the point. Amazing. Simply amazing. Now let's get back to the story on this 23rd not long ago. I had a really, complicated frustrating day. I was laying in the bed pouting when my baby came home. I needed him so bad right now. Not his dick this time. I needed his heart. You have heard about how he loves my body, but this is the foundation of why I submit to my baby.

He hears me sobbing and puts something down that he is carrying then turns on the light. He grabbed me and held me so freaking tight, but he does not say a word. I don't know how, it's like he just knew. I didn't need him to talk to me, just hold me and let me cry on him. When I tell you, I cried so hard and for so long. I could feel my tears rolling down face and snot dripping from my nose onto him. Not once did he move, he continued to hold me close squeezing me tighter and tighter. The more I cried I could just feel the stress and worry slip away. I stopped sobbing and went in our bathroom to clean my face. When I walked back into the room, I pulled the wet rag from my face and something catches my attention in the corner. It is red and it is big. I am like what is that? The closer I get; I can tell that it is a plush animal half my size. When I pick the bag up and pull it out and see that it is a fox. I will name her Foxy. I hug and say thanks to my baby. I am about to hug him when I see the flowers that were behind the bag. They are the most beautiful red roses I have ever seen. I reach for them and smell them as he walks up behind me. He kisses my neck, and I sit the roses back down. I lean back turn my face and kiss him as I gab the back of his head. I say I don't know how you even knew but I really, really, needed this. Thank You…

Now, I know ya'll did not think I would end this book like that. He walks me over to the bed and lays me down slowly. He eases my clothes off as he is kissing me and rubbing all over me at the same time. Teasing me the way I love the most It is my favorite part. It drives me insane. It's hard to explain. He is touching me, but he is not touching me. His energy is pulsating from his hand through my body. As he continues to rub my body he says, "Let Mr. Daddy rub that stress away." While he is massaging me, I can feel his finger sliding slightly between my booty cheeks. Next, I feel his lips kissing my booty as I begin to tremble and shake. "Uh huh look a there I got you trembling and shaking girl." Then he takes his clothes off as he watches me squirm and moan still trembling and shaking cumming all over myself uncontrollably. I roll over so I can watch him get naked.

God, I love his body. I crawl to the bottom of the bed and start sucking him off. Upside down laying on my back. Now I am in the perfect spot to suck his dick and balls at the same time, one of his favorites. So, as I am going in, he is rubbing and kissing licking and sucking me back. I pull him all the way down on to me. And let him fuck my face, until I gag choking myself. I don't why but this always makes me cum.

Now he is slurping my juices. I am screaming "No, No, No, Ok baby ok baby ok baby." He finally gets up and gets on to of me putting my legs on his shoulder teasing my clit making me squirt, sliding it in between my lips. First the head, now the whole thing. The deeper he sinks into me the tighter our bodies get to each other. It feels like we are one. It hurts so bad, but I don't want him to stop. His hands are gripping my shoulders and he is pulling, deeper, deeper than anybody has ever gone before. He is opening dimensions that I didn't know exist. How is that possible? He chokes me and sticks his tongue in my mouth as he keeps pumping at a steady pace. Clap, Clap, Clap, Clap, is all we hear as he drives in again and again and again. My eyes are rolling back in my head and I am speaking gibberish again or in tongues or something. Anyway, I don't know what planet I am on right now. The shape of his dick has carved my walls to his custom fit.

Being faithful has so many marvelous benefits. He gives me all of him and I give him all of me. Know one knows me better than he does. No one has ever treated me better than he does. He makes me feel adored, secure, wanted and sexy every day of my life. He showers me with attention, gifts, affection, kisses and compliments. I know his heart is mine and I take pride in it. I cherish his heart as much as I do his body. He makes me feel like I am a living breathing diamond.

I love our love. The sex is out of this world but that is just the icing on the love cake. Now back to the sex……. Sike!!! I was just playing. All good things must come to an end. I truly, truly, truly appreciate you all. So, until the next 23 Ways of Sex Play, be happy, pray, and don't forget to suck your man's dick every day.

To be continued…….

XOXOXO

10 Reasons Why I Love You

10 Reasons Why I Love Chevella

1. You are dependable. No matter what happens good or bad I know that you always will be here to share my successes or setbacks.
2. Your positive words of encouragement remind me that I have the power to create the life that I want to live.
3. Your pretty face and smile bring me joy every time I look at you. I love looking at you.
4. You listen to me and do whatever I ask you to do. I love that shit.
5. You learn from your mistakes and you make changes to avoid doing the same things again. I love your mind.
6. You take care of my stomach, mind, body, heart and spirit. Your food gives my power to do the impossible. You protect my heart from stress. Please and soothe my body. Your love lifts my spirit. You got my back.
7. You always look like you are so happy to see me. I feel wanted when you look at me. I enjoy turning you out. I love your desire for me.
8. Your body is so, so beautiful. I love the way you react to my touch and the sound of my voice. I love how you surrender to me and give complete control of you. I love the way you feel inside and out.

9. You are the nicest, most generous, and thoughtful person that I have ever met. You have survived more pain and disappointment than any one I have ever met, but you continue to love people no matter what. I feel safe that you won't break my heart because your love is truly real.
10. You have vision drive and grit just like me. You know life is hard, so you fight hard for what you want in life and you make me do the same. The confidence that you give me by believing in me makes us unstoppable. And we can do anything and everything.

10 Reasons Why I Love Virgil

1. You are the very first person and only person who has ever called me gorgeous. You make feel it, believe it, see it and you make me own that shit.

2. The bond that you share with our kids. Nothing could ever compare to that; the way it makes my heart feel when I see ya'll interact.

3. You're the most hardest working dependable and taking pride in every single thing you do. From being a son brother father but most of all my man. That takes hard work. Thanks….

4. OMG, I can't believe I didn't start with your words. Baby, the things you say to me and also show me they're true. When you open up to me in a poem card or even a song, WOW is all I can say. Your words still take my breath away.

5. You can always, always, always I mean always make me smile. One simple touch kiss or even a look. Yep I'm hooked that smile got me. Because I love your smile.

6. I love the way you carry yourself like a BOSS at all times. You walk tall like you are in control of everything and everyone around you, always. You never ever half ass do anything, you always give it your best. I don't know where you find the strength most days. Amazing…

7. Your style is definitely one of a kind, that's why I am glad you're are mine all mine. I love to watch you cut your hair and shave. I love seeing you dressed in OG mode, so damn clean, like a pimp, and rock the crowd at our shows. I am your #1 fan, on and off the stage and I always will be. So please keep making love to your number one fan.
8. The fact that you can give me a whole orgasm without any penetration is so damn CRAZY!
9. You can make love to me with your thoughts, you can read my mind. You control my whole well-being. You turn me out on a daily basis. Man, I love me some you.
10. Because of you I am a better mother, friend, lover as well as a better woman overall. I was lost without you. I did not love me, now thanks to you, I adore me. You loving me, made me love me.

Team Get Money
We are Beautiful, Bold and Unstoppable.
AUTISM AWARENESS PARENTS

I am Saint Villo DeVille. She is Queen Love. And together we are "Team Get Money". We are a very in love young black power couple. We are the first couple to ever do stand-up comedy on stage together. We are getting married as soon as we buy our big house. We have a play and talk show called "Anything and Everything". This means that we play music and video clips then we talk about how the art relates to our lives as well as our listeners lives and current issues in the world.

We start the show interviewing other people as we all eat meals from the local restaurants and bistros live on air. Some shows we may cook our own meals live on the show. Then we rate the food and tell our audience where to go to find the real good food in and around Atlanta. We may cook our own meals live on the show depending on our set's capabilities. We may have kids and adult guests appear on our show each episode.

After we eat, we will dance to a few songs, then we sit back down to continue the interviews. In the interviews we let business owners tell their story and promote themselves. We let kids and adults express their concerns and interests with the world. Anything and Everything is open for discussion on our show. We give everybody including artists, poets and comedians a platform to reach a new fan base. We are Public Motivational Speakers and Autism Awareness Advocates who enjoy entertaining, informing and educating our audience.

We are outstanding entertainers, actors, radio talk show hosts, caterers, electricians, massage therapists, artists and models plus much more. If you search Google for Saint Villo DeVille or Search YouTube for Saint Villo Deville or Anything and Everything you will see our stand-up comedy and concerts and hear Saint Villo DeVille's music. We are looking for a new platform. It could be in a studio or on location.

I have a good rapport with a large data base of guests that will be thrilled to come on our show to be interviewed.

My contacts range from entertainers, athletes, to educators, to entrepreneurs, as well as politicians, lawyers and doctors. We will end each show with Team Get Money doing a comedy skit or a concert performance.

Our show shines the spotlight on hidden talent, good locally owned businesses and the issues that affect us all.......

The Anything and Everything Show with "Team Get Money."

        404-246-8909   Virgil Lindsey/Saint Villo DeVille

        404-587-5833   Chevella Dyer/ Queen Love

        reddyer28@gmail.com

        saintvillodeville@gmail.com

https://www.youtube.com/results?search_query=saint+villo+deville

https://soundcloud.com/search?q=saint%20villo%20deville

Acknowledgments

First and foremost, I would like to give honor to the most- high and my mommy. Thank you, guys for making me. Without you there would be no me.

To my wonderful and amazing other- half and co-author, Virgil Lindsey. THANKS for seeing me, when I couldn't see me. I was so lost without you. Thank GOD the universe allowed us to find each other. Now you complete me. I love you.

To my children, I want to say Thanks to all four of you. Ty, India, King and Angel, keep doing you and being amazing at it. I love you. You guys are freaking awesome.

To myself, for being brave and bold and having the courage to write this book.

www.ingramcontent.com/pod-product-compliance
Lightning Source LLC
Chambersburg PA
CBHW021025090426
42738CB00007B/912